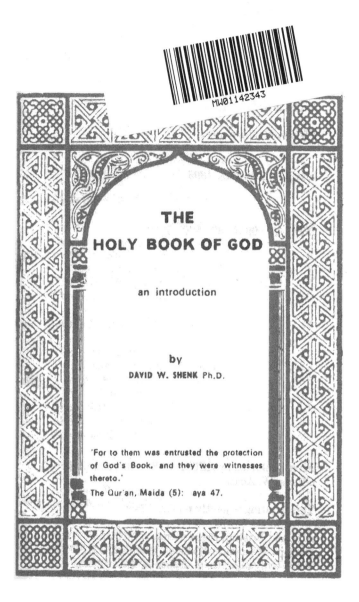

THE
HOLY BOOK OF GOD

an introduction

by

DAVID W. SHENK Ph.D.

'For to them was entrusted the protection
of God's Book, and they were witnesses
thereto.'
The Qur'an, Maida (5): aya 47.

1

First publication 1981

Second publication 1995

Third publication 2015
Cover photo credit: Caleb Bornman

First published by ACP, P.O. Box 30,
Achimota Ghana, W. Africa.

Table of Contents

Preface *5*

Introduction *6*

1: The Holy Scriptures *8*

The Spoken and Living Word *8*

The Acts of God *10*

God's Acts in Creation *10*

God's Acts in History *11*

The Main Divisions of the Holy Scriptures *13*

The Science of Examination *16*

2: The Old Testament *20*

The Torah (Taurat) *20*

The Writings and the Prophets *23*

The Writings *23*

The Prophets *24*

The Reliability of the Text *26*

Ancient Manuscripts *29*

Trustworthy Scriptures *34*

3: The New Testament *36*

Apostolic writings *36*

When it was written..*38*

The formation of the New Testament *40*

The Gospel (Injil)...*42*

The Acts and Epistles *44*

Divine Inspiration *46*

Ancient Manuscripts *48*

Trustworthy Scriptures..*51*

4: Translations *57*

Conclusion *60*

Appendix A...*62*

Comments from the Qur'an concerning the Bible62

Appendix B...*66*

The history of the Holy Book of God *66*

For further reading..*67*

End Notes...*69*

Preface

Sheikh Abdulquadir is a devout man of God and a dear personal friend. We frequently share together about faith in God.

A question which the Sheikh asks me is this: Have you who are People of the Book ever changed the Scriptures which God has entrusted to your keeping?

That is a good question. It is a vital question which both Muslims and Christians confront whenever they talk together about revelation.

In this booklet I have tried to respond to the Sheikh's question.

As I have written, I have sensed the tremendous significance of the Qur'anic command:

"0 people of the book! Ye have no ground to stand upon unless you stand fast by the Law *(Taurat)* and the Gospel *(Injil)* and all the revelation that has come to you from your Lord"

The Qur'an: Maida (5): aya 71.

Introduction

Muslims recognize that Jews and Christians are 'The People of the Book" (The Qur'an: Maida (5): aya 68).

The Qur'an shows great respect for the Holy Book of God which is called the Bible. This is because the Qur'an teaches that the Holy Writings of the Bible have been revealed by God. The Qur'an says:

> ". . . He (Allah) sent down the Law (*Taurat* of the prophet Moses), and the Gospel (*Injil* of Jesus the Messiah)" (Ali Imran (3): aya 3).

Muslims also recognize that God has commanded the People of the book to preserve His revelation. We read in the Qur'an: "For to them was entrusted the protection of God's Book ..." (Maida (5): aya 47). And later in the same Sura we read, "0 People of the Book, you have no ground to stand upon unless you stand fast by the Law *(Taurat)* and the Gospel *(Injil)* and all the revelation that has come to you from your Lord" (Maida (5): aya 71).

Christians are thankful that Islam teaches great respect for the Holy Book of God, which is called the Bible.

This book is dedicated to Sheikh Abdulqadir who seeks to submit to the will of Allah.

> 'Oh, how I love Thy Law!
> It is my meditation all the day.'

-The *Zabur* (Psalms) of the Prophet David

Qur'anic quotations are from the publication of Dar al Arabia Publishing Printing and Distribution, Beirut.

Biblical quotations are from the *Revised Standard Version*, copyrighted 1946 and 1952.

1: The Holy Scriptures

'Thy Word is a lamp to my feet and a light to my path." The *Zabur* of the Prophet David (Psalm 119:105).

More Bibles are sold around the world each year than any other book. In many countries the favourite book for reading is the Bible.

Why do millions of people from many different countries desire to buy and read the Bible? Why is the Bible such a wonderful book?

The Bible itself gives an answer. The Bible says, "All Scripture is inspired by God," (2 Timothy 3:16). The word 'inspire' means to breathe into. In other words, the Bible has been written by holy men of God into whom God breathed His thoughts. (Hebrews 4:12)

The Spoken and Living Word

There are two important ways in which the Bible is the Word of God:

(1) God revealed His thoughts to the prophets *(nebi)* and apostles *(rusul)*. Many of the prophets said that they "saw" the Word of the Lord (Isaiah 1:1, Obadiah 1:1, Micah 1:1, Habakkuk 1:1). The Word of the Lord which the prophets "saw" or "heard" was written down.

As the prophets "saw" or "heard" the Word of God, they proclaimed that Word. Sometimes the holy prophets themselves wrote down the Word which God revealed; the Taurat says that God commanded the Prophet Moses to write the words of the covenant

(Exodus 34:27-28). More often the disciples and faithful secretaries wrote the Word of God as they heard it from the mouth of the holy prophet. We read, for example, that the scribe Baruch wrote on a scroll at the dictation of the Prophet Jeremiah "all the Word of the Lord which he had spoken to him" (Jeremiah 36:4). The Bible consists of the Holy Writings which have come through God's revelation to the prophets.

(2) The Bible also reveals to us the life and teachings of Jesus the Messiah, who is the Living Word of God (*Kalimatuhu*). The prophets of God from Adam (Genesis 3:15), to the Prophet Abraham (Genesis 22:18), to the Prophet Moses (Deuteronomy 18:15), to the Prophet David (2 Samuel 7:12-13), to the Prophet Malachi (Malachi 4:2), recognized that the Messiah would be God's full and special revelation to humankind. When the Messiah came, the apostles (*rusul* of God) who were with Him recognized that Jesus the Messiah is the Word of God in human form.

The Gospel (Injil) says, "In the beginning was the Word, and the Word was with God; . . . And the Word became flesh and dwelt among us, full of grace and truth" (John 1:1, 2, 14).

The Qur'an also speaks of the Messiah as the Word of God *(kalimatuhu) (Nis Jesus aa (4):171.)*

The Holy Writings of God find their true meaning and value in the life and teachings of the Messiah, who is the Living Word of God. Jesus the Messiah is the center and fulfillment of all the Holy Writings of God.

-- The Messiah says: The Scriptures "... bear witness to Me"

(John 5:39).

Again He says: "If you believed Moses, you would believe Me, for he wrote of Me. But if you do not believe his writings, how will you believe My words?" (John 5:46, 47)

The holy prophets *spoke* the Word of God. Jesus the Messiah *is* the Living Word of God.

The Bible is God's Word because it contains both the Holy Writings of the Prophets *and* the record of the life and teachings of the Messiah, who is Himself the Living Word of God.

The Acts of God

The Word of God shows us that God chose to reveal Himself to humankind. God reveals Himself by what He does and by the interpretation of His acts by His inspired prophets and apostles. Creation and history are two areas where God's actions can be seen.

God's Acts in Creation

Creation is a sign of divine revelation. The scientists, who explore the mysteries of birth, life, wind, rain, sun, plant life, or the stars, help us understand how wonderfully and carefully God has created the heavens and the earth.

> The Qur'an also speaks of creation as signs from God. "Behold! In the creation of the heavens and the earth. And the alternation of Night and Day,-- There are indeed Signs for men of understanding"(Ali Imran (3): 3).

The beauty of the sunrise, the mystery of life, the life-giving power of rain--God has carefully and lovingly created! In the Psalms (*Zabur*) of the Prophet David we read:

"0 give thanks to the Lord, for He is good, For His steadfast love endures forever ...
To Him Who alone does great wonders ...
To Him Who by understanding made the heavens...
To Him Who spread out the earth upon the waters...
To Him Who made the great lights ...
The sun to rule over the day...
The moon and stars to rule over the night ..."
(Psalm 136:1, 4-9).

God does reveal something about Himself through creation!

God's Acts in History

Because God is at work in human affairs, history also reveals something about God. Although God is at work in all nations everywhere, it is especially through the people of faith that His actions are most evident. Within the Bible we learn that the people who responded in faith to God were invited into a covenant relationship with God.*

This new community of people who believed in God was the People of the Covenant. God's acts in history were especially and wonderfully evident in the life and experience of the People of the Covenant: God delivered them from slavery. He divided the waters of the Red Sea so that they could cross on dry land. He revealed His Law (the *Taurat*) to them at Mount Sinai. He fed them in the desert for forty years. It gave them a good land for cattle and farming. The Bible contains the historical record of the

* The covenant is an agreement of blessing between God and the people of faith.

wonderful acts of God on behalf of the People of the Covenant.

God's actions in history are the central part of His revelation to humankind. It is for this reason that the Bible includes the history of the People of the Covenant. God revealed to the prophets the meaning of His actions on behalf of the Covenant. Therefore the Bible consists of both the history of the People of the Covenant and the interpretation of that history which God revealed through His holy prophets.

The Bible includes both a description of God's actions in history and the Word of revelation through prophets and apostles. Both are revelation. Therefore an accurate record of the history of the People of God is just as important as is an accurate record of the Word which the prophets 'saw' or 'heard.' It is for this reason that the Holy Scriptures include:

(1) The affirmation of God's action as Creator and an account of God's deeds in history.

(2) The interpretation of His acts as revealed through the holy prophets and apostles.

(3) The life and teachings of the Messiah who is the Living Word of God.

These three basic aspects of God's revelation form the Holy Scriptures which are the Bible.

The Main Divisions of the Holy Scriptures

In the Bible there are two main parts known as the Old Testament and the New Testament. Another word for Testament is Covenant or Solemn Agreement. The Old Testament was written before the Messiah had come, and the New Testament was written after the Messiah had come.

In the Old Testament or Old Covenant we learn that God made a covenant with the People of Israel at the time when He gave them the Ten Commandments at Mount Sinai just after they had been freed by God from slavery under Pharaoh. Tragically, the People of Israel often failed to obey God. God was faithful, but they were not. They turned away from God and did not respect the covenant which God had made with them.

> The Qur'an also speaks of the covenant God made with the People of Israel and the manner in which they failed to obey God. The Qur'an says: "And remember we took a covenant from the children of Israel: ...Then did ye turn back, except for a few among you" *(Baqara* (2): 83).

The People of the Covenant slowly came to recognize that the Old Covenant was a preparation for a new and better covenant. God revealed through the prophets that the Old Covenant was a sign or a shadow of a better covenant which God would reveal through the Messiah.

The Prophet Jeremiah spoke of the New Covenant in this way:

> Behold, the days are coming, says the Lord, when I will make a new covenant with the house of Israel and the house of Judah, not like the covenant which I made

with their fathers when I took them by the hand to bring them out of the land of Egypt, my covenant which they broke, though I was their husband, says the Lord. But this is the covenant which I will make with the house of Israel after those days, says the Lord: I will put My Law within them, and I will write it upon their hearts; and I will be their God, and they shall be my people. And no longer shall each man teach his neighbor and each his brother, saying, "Know the Lord," for they shall all know Me, from the least of 'them to the greatest, says the Lord; for I will forgive their iniquity, and I will remember their sin no more ' (Jeremiah 31:31-34).

The New Testament describes God's New Covenant with humankind, a covenant which is based on the life, death and resurrection of Jesus the Messiah, a covenant of salvation and eternal life. The New Covenant is a new creation in the lives of people, a miracle of grace, forgiveness, and power which enables people to give themselves in self-giving, joyous love just as the Messiah gave Himself in love for all people.

The- New Covenant is a fulfillment of the Old Covenant; that is to say, the Old Testament looks forward to the coming of the Messiah, and the New Testament is the record of the manner in which God has completed that which was not complete in the Old Covenant. The Old Covenant with its laws and regulations for right worship was a 'copy and shadow ' (Hebrews 8:5) of the New Covenant which the Messiah has established. This means that in order to understand the New Covenant we need to recognize that the Old Covenant was a preparation for the New.

The Old Covenant is similar to the full moon shining in the night, and the New Covenant is similar to the sun. Although we enjoy walking in the full moon, its light is not sufficient for us to see the path ahead clearly. The moon is a sign that day time will come, that the sun will appear in the morning; when the morning sun rises from the east, suddenly all the earth is filled with brightness. The night time moon which reflects the light of the sun is good, but we see much better when walking in the direct light of the sun. In a similar way the Old Covenant was a reflection and a sign of the brightness of the New Covenant which God has established through the Messiah.

Jesus the Messiah recognized that He was the fulfillment of the Old Testament. He said, "You search the Scriptures (Old Testament), because you think that in them you have eternal life; and it is they that bear witness to Me" (John 5:39). Nevertheless, the Messiah never considered setting aside the Old Testament. He said, "Think not that I have come to abolish the law and prophets; I have not come to abolish them, but to fulfill them" (Matthew 5:17).

> The Qur'an also shows that the Messiah confirmed the Old Testament Scriptures. We read: "I have come to you to attest the Law which was before me" (Ali Imran (3): 50).

The Messiah told His disciples that the Old Testament must be fulfilled. He said, ' I say to you, till heaven and earth pass away, not an iota, not a dot, will pass from the Law until all is accomplished ' (Matthew 5:18). The Messiah warned that anyone who attempts to change the Law of Moses will be least in the Kingdom of God (Matthew 5:19).

The great respect which Jesus the Messiah had for the Old Testament is revealed in the way He quoted from the writings of the Prophet Moses, the Prophet David, and other prophets. In His sermons He often stood on the authority of the Old Testament Scriptures.

15

When Satan came to tempt the Messiah, He put Satan to flight by quoting the *Taurat* of the Prophet Moses (Matthew 4:1-11). He used the Old Testament to explain and interpret His mission to the people of His day. Similarly, in the early Church the apostles of God who were disciples of Jesus the Messiah used the Old Testament Scriptures constantly in their sermons and teaching.

Today Christians everywhere accept both the Old Testament and the New Testament as the Holy Writings of God. The Old Testament is a preparation for the coming of the Messiah. The New Testament is the account of the coming of the Messiah and the work He began. The Old Covenant is a sign of the New Covenant. In order to understand the New, we must also understand the Old. Therefore the Bible contains both the Old Testament and the New Testament.

The Science of Examination

Throughout the history of the Church scholars have attempted to examine the Scriptures to try to understand the deeper meaning of the texts and also to determine whether the text is accurate, that it is the same as the original writings. This method of textual examination is called Biblical criticism. The term Biblical criticism refers to the careful and scientific study of the texts of the Bible. Biblical examination has developed into a very respectable science which draws on information from archeology, linguistics, history, culture and textual comparison.

There are two kinds of attitudes which people bring to Biblical examination. One attitude examines the Bible without any concern for faith in God or the message which the Bible contains. The other type of Biblical examination comes from faith in God and His revelation. It attempts to understand the text more deeply so that the message of the Bible can speak more effectively. Both kinds of Biblical examination use similar kinds of scientific tools, but the assumptions are different in the two kinds of scholars.

Origen is the father of Biblical examination. His method of Bible study is an example of Biblical criticism which believes in God and the Holy Scriptures. He was an African who lived most of his life in Alexandria, Egypt (AD. 185 to 253). He was a brilliant theologian, who at the age of only eighteen became head of the first Christian University, the Alexandrian Catechetical School. Origen was a specialist in Biblical studies. He developed an excellent method of textual study to determine whether Greek translations of the Hebrew Old Testament Scriptures were accurate.

Origen did his textual study by comparing the original Hebrew Old Testament text, the Hebrew text in Greek letters, and four Greek translations of the Hebrew Scriptures; all of these were written in six parallel columns. For this reason Origen's document was called the Hexapla, meaning six- fold. Origen used this method to compare the various texts, and in this way he could determine whether there were any mistakes in the translations.

The Hexapla represented a tremendous amount of work; it took Origen and as many as fourteen secretaries twenty-five years to complete it. The excellent method of textual examination which Origen developed in the Hexapla is often used by Biblical scholars even today.

On the other hand, Celsus is an example of a student of the Bible whose approach to Biblical criticism does not encourage belief in the Holy Scriptures. Celsus lived in Palestine in the later second century, A.D., and he studied the Scriptures critically, but with a different intention from Origen. Celsus wanted to destroy faith in the Biblical

17

message. He did this by trying to discover contradictions between what different prophets had spoken.

As already mentioned, there have always been some scholars who examine the Bible without faith and others who study it through the eyes of faith. Both kinds of scholars use similar types of scientific tools in their study of the Bible, but they interpret their findings differently. We should always remember this when we read the interpretations of Biblical examination. At the same time we need to recognize that most Biblical examination throughout the twentieth century has been moving toward a greater appreciation for the accuracy and reliability of the Biblical texts as we have them today.

This shift in viewpoint is demonstrated by comparing the German 19th century scholar, Julius Wellhausen, with the 20th century American scholar, William Foxwell Albright. Wellhausen lived during a time when the theory of evolution was very popular. Consequently, Wellhausen tried to interpret the Old Testament and the New Testament for an evolutionary and almost atheistic point of view. He tried to support the view that the Bible represented a gradual evolution in the religious thinking of the People of God which had little or nothing to do with revelation. In other words, he believed that the Bible was the word of man rather the Word of God.

Today most Biblical scholars reject Wellhausen's viewpoint. In fact, Albright, one of the greatest archeological scholars of all time, says that the old theory that the Bible is the result of religious evolution has been demonstrated as an "impossibility."[1] This is to say that modern archeological studies have shown that the Bible is not part of an overall religious evolution, but rather a new and radically different way of life and belief which was not to be found anywhere else in the ancient Middle East.

Why is the Bible so different? The believer is persuaded that the reason lies in the nature of God's unique revelation to humankind through the prophets and the Messiah. The believer is also confident that whenever people read the Bible with an open, prayerful spirit, God will reveal to that person that the Holy Writings are truly the Word of God.

Now we need to examine how the Old Testament and New Testament came to be. We also need to determine whether we can be confident in the trustworthiness of our modern copies of these ancient Scriptures which have been transmitted to us through hundreds of years.

Questions

(1) Who is the Living Word of God?

(2) Compare the Old Testament and the New Testament.

(3) Why does the Bible contain the account of the history of the Covenant People?

(4) Contrast the approach to Biblical criticism used by Origen and Celsus.

2: The Old Testament

"Forever, 0 Lord, Thy Word is firmly fixed in the heavens."
The *Zabur* of the Prophet David (Psalm 119:89).

Our study of the Old Testament deals in general with two
main concerns: (1) How the original text came to be
written. (2) Whether the text we have today is an accurate
transmission of the original text.

The Torah *(Taurat)*

The opening Scriptures of the Old Testament are the first
five books which are collectively known as the Torah
(Taurat) of the Prophet Moses. The names of these books
are Genesis, Exodus, Leviticus, Numbers, and
Deuteronomy. These five books are called the Pentateuch.
("Penta" means "five" and "teuch" means "book.") They
are considered to have been mostly written by the Prophet
Moses.

> The Qur'an speaks of the books of Abraham and Moses is
> the earliest written revelation. (Ala (87):18, 19). The
> Taurat of the Prophet Moses includes God's revelation to
> the Prophet Abraham (Genesis 11:31-25:8).

The Prophet Moses was not the only man of God whose
life is included in these Holy Writings.

Abraham, Ishmael, Isaac, Jacob, Joseph, Moses, and the
Priest and Prophet Aaron are all important men of God
who are included in the *Taurat*.

A significant portion of the *Taurat* includes the account of the life and teachings of the Prophet Abraham. Some Biblical scholars believe that the revelation in the *Taurat* which relates particularly to the Prophet Abraham uses the term El or Elohim for God. This is because Abraham knew God as El or Elohim, which is the Hebrew form of the Arabic name for God, Allah. The revelation of God through Abraham is largely included in the first portion of the *Taurat* which is called Genesis.

However, the largest portion of the *Taurat* is a record of God's revelation through the Prophet Moses. [2] In the *Taurat* we read that the Prophet Moses himself wrote portions of the *Taurat* as it was revealed to him by God:

> "And the Lord said to Moses, "Write these words; in accordance with these words I have made a covenant with you and with Israel." And he was there with the Lord forty days and forty nights; he neither ate bread nor drank water. And he wrote upon the tables the words of the covenant, the ten commandments" (Exodus 34:27-28).

> 'And Moses wrote this law, and gave it to the priests the sons of Levi, who carried the ark of the covenant of the Lord and to all the elders of Israel ' (Deuteronomy 31:9).

It is not surprising that the Prophet Moses himself wrote portions of the *Taurat*. He was a highly educated man, probably trained in the Egyptian University of Heliopolis. Certainly anything which Moses wrote would have been carefully preserved by his disciples.

God's revelation to the Prophet Moses began at a burning bush in the Sinai Desert when God appeared to Moses and commanded him to lead the Hebrew people out of slavery under: Pharaoh. At that time God gave the Prophet Moses

21

a new name for Himself. God said that His name is "I Am."
The Hebrew word for "I Am" is Yahweh. In much of the
Taurat the Prophet Moses uses the name "Yahweh" for the
Covenant God.

The great Prophet of the *Taurat* is the Prophet Moses. In
fact, the Prophet Moses is one of the greatest prophets of
the entire Old Testament. Although many prophets are
mentioned in the Old Testament, and God's revelation
through more than thirty prophets is included in the Old
Testament, one writer after another in the Old Testament -
- and even the Messiah Himself -- referred to the writings
of the Prophet Moses; the *Taurat* of the Prophet Moses is
indeed the key to an understanding of the entire Old
Testament.

> The Qur'an refers to the writings of Moses as the criterion
> (*furqan)* of truth. *(Anbiyaa* (21):48 and *Baqara (*2):53.) It
> is called a guidance, a light, a mercy, the Book of Allah.
> *(Maida (*5): 47, *Hud* (11): 17, *Anbiyaa (*21):48.)

Holy men of God who were disciples and followers of the
Prophet Moses carefully preserved the writings and
teachings of the holy prophet and organized these writings
in an orderly manner. These writings were organized into
the five books of the *Taurat*: Genesis is about the
beginnings of humankind. Exodus is about the deliverance
of the People of the Covenant from slavery under the
Pharaoh. Leviticus is a record of God's laws concerning
right worship. Numbers is about the organization of the
People of the Covenant. Deuteronomy is a summary and
explanation of all God's laws which were revealed at
Mount Sinai.

We are confident that those who combined and organized
these Holy Scriptures into the five divisions of the *Taurat*
were careful to preserve accurately all the divinely
inspired writings, teachings, and historical accounts. We

believe that God who revealed Himself so marvelously to the Prophet Moses and the People of the Covenant, also preserved the account of his revelation and guided those who organized the Holy Scriptures into its five divisions or books.

Muslim scholars describe the organization of the Qur'an into 114 *Suras* during the reign of Caliph Othman. Although the arrangement of the Qur'an in its present form did not happen until several years after it had been recited, Muslim scholars are confident that the text itself is a reliable record of the original recitations.

The Writings and the Prophets

The Holy *Taurat* is not the only Scripture revealed in the Old Testament. There are also the Writings and the Prophets. The Writings include books on the history of the People of the Covenant and poetry. The Prophets include the Major Prophets and the Minor Prophets.

The Writings

The Writings are the largest portion of the Old Testament. The Historical Writings interpret the history of the People of the Covenant through the experience of faith in God. These historical books are fascinating descriptions of the great political upheavals which Palestine experienced as a buffer state between great African empires and the Mesopotamian empires.

In all these great and tragic events the Hebrew historians saw and interpreted the activity of God in their history. For this reason we recognize that the historical books of the Old Testament are not ordinary history. They are the faith interpretation of God's actions in the history of the

Covenant People. The history books of the Old Testament are Joshua, Judges, Ruth, 1 and 2 Samuel, 1 and 2 Kings, 1 and 2 Chronicles, Ezra, Nehemiah, Esther.

The Writings which are poetry include Job, Psalms, Proverbs, Song of Solomon, and Ecclesiastes. Of these books of poetry the Psalms (*Zabur*) are best known and greatly loved. The *Zabur* were inspired by God and many were written by the Prophet and king named David. Jesus the Messiah often quoted from the *Zabur*. These poems represent some of the finest Hebrew poetry ever written.

Interestingly, David's son Solomon was also a poet, and his Song of Solomon is a love poem which many people interpret allegorically to be a description of the love of God for humankind. Others see it as a beautiful description of God's gift of love in the marriage relationship.

The Prophets

The third portion of the Old Testament is The Prophets. All of the Old Testament has come to us through the inspired prophets of God, but the portion of the Old Testament which is called ' The Prophets, ' was revealed at a time when the People of the Covenant were experiencing intense difficulty. The faith of the people was declining. Enemies were invading the land, and finally the whole nation was taken into captivity to Babylon (sixth century B.C.).

It was during this tragic time that God blessed the People of the Covenant in a special way by sending many prophets to them who ' saw ' the Word of the Lord and proclaimed that Word to the people. Some of these prophets wrote down what God had revealed to them; in other cases they proclaimed the Word of the Lord, and faithful disciples and scribes wrote down what they said.

The books of the Prophets are as follows: Isaiah, Jeremiah, Lamentations, Ezekiel, Daniel, Hosea, Joel, Amos, Obadiah, Jonah, Micah, Nahum, Habakkuk, Zephaniah, Haggai, Zechariah, Malachi.

One of the greatest prophets during this time was Isaiah. The Prophet Isaiah foresaw in a profound way that the coming Messiah would establish a New Covenant between God and people which would become a blessing to all humankind. He saw that in order to establish the New Covenant the Messiah would suffer and give his life for the sins of the people.

It was probably during the fifth century B.C. that the portions of the Old Testament known as the Writings and the Prophets were collected and organized in the form in which we have them today. Ancient tradition says that the Priest of God, Ezra, was inspired by God to collect these Holy Writings and organize them into books.

It seems that a general agreement developed between 300 and 200 B.C. concerning the list of books which are included in the Old Testament. A list of thirty-nine books was accepted as the inspired Word of God. All these thirty-nine books or Scripture portions are contained in the Holy Scriptures of the *Taurat*, the Writings and the Prophets; together they form the Old Testament Scriptures. We are confident that the holy people of God who determined which books to include in the Old Testament were led by God to accept only those Holy Writings which had been inspired by God.

We have already mentioned that Jesus the Messiah accepted the Old Testament as the Word of God. He based His message and preaching on the Old Testament. The Messiah knew the Old Testament thoroughly, and He often quoted from these sacred Scriptures in His sermons and teaching. He quoted the Holy Writings of many of the

Prophets of God such as Moses, Isaiah, Jeremiah, Ezekiel, Daniel, Micah, Hosea, Malachi and others.

It is obvious that Jesus the Messiah accepted the Old Testament as inspired by God and as authoritative Scripture which possessed an eternal message. All who accept Jesus as the Messiah should certainly show the same respect for the Scriptures as Jesus showed.

The Reliability of the Text

The Old Testament texts were first written in Hebrew, the native tongue of the People of the Covenant. These Holy Writings of God were recorded during a span of more than 40 generations; from the time that the Prophet Moses received the revelation from God at Mount Sinai until the time of the last prophets of the Old Testament, is a period of at least 1,000 years. Probably the last prophetic revelations of the Old Testament were recorded about 300 B.C., nearly 2,300 years ago. How can we be confident that these ancient Holy Scriptures have not been corrupted?

There are several reasons why Biblical scholars do much research to see whether the Old Testament as we have it today is the same as the original Hebrew text.

First, the original Hebrew was written only in consonants. The Hebrew alphabet had no vowels. So Hebrew writing would have looked something like this: 'n th bgnnng gd crtd th hvns nd th rth.' Can you understand that sentence? It is the first verse in the *Taurat* which reads: "In the beginning God created the heavens and the earth."

Hebrew scholars can readily read the ancient Hebrew even though it is without vowel marks, but sometimes there is a word which is a problem, for it might mean one word or another word. For example, 'fn' might mean 'fin' or 'fun' or 'fan.' By studying the context the scholars are usually able to be sure what the word is, but we need to recognize that an alphabet without vowel marks can be perplexing sometimes.

> The Arabic and Hebrew alphabets have some similarities. In ancient times both alphabets used only consonants without any vowel signs. The earliest Qur'anic Arabic manuscripts were also written without vowel signs just as was true of the ancient Hebrew manuscripts of the Old Testament.

The second question arises because all the ancient texts needed to be copied by hand. This has been true of all scriptures of all peoples everywhere. It was only in the 15th century A.D. that printing began to be widely used, and until that time all Bibles had been copied by hand. For nearly 2,000 years all Old Testament texts were handwritten copies! We know that when someone is copying written words by hand, it is possible to make mistakes.

Biblical scholars try to discover any mistakes which might have crept into the Old Testament writings because of errors made by the people who were copying those texts by hand from one manuscript to another. Fortunately the various copyists did not make the same mistakes! Therefore, by comparing many ancient manuscripts, scholars can determine with great accuracy the exact words of the original text.

A third matter which the scholars investigate is whether any deliberate alterations or changes have been introduced into the Old Testament during the process of its transmission to us.

Biblical scholars use all the linguistic and archeological tools available to determine the precise meaning of a given word or thought in the early Hebrew text. In spite of the three problems we have listed (alphabet without vowel signs, hand-copied manuscripts, possible manuscript alterations) scholars have established much evidence of the careful preservation of these Holy Scriptures. We can note only three in this short discussion.

First, archeology has shown that the historical events described in the Holy *Taurat* are accurate. In fact the Old Testament is the most accurate history book written by ancient peoples, which is in existence today.[3]

For example, the *Taurat* describes in considerable detail the life and culture of the Prophet Abraham, including certain historical events which took place during his life time. Archeology and the discovery of some ancient fragments of writing in Mesopotamia and Egypt have shown that these biblical accounts are accurate.

Another example is a fragment of a letter sent by the King of Canaan about 1,300 B.C. requesting help from Pharaoh of Egypt because the *Habiru* had begun to invade the land. This is an apparent reference to the beginnings of the Hebrew invasions of Palestine which are so fascinatingly described in Joshua, the first book of The Writings.

A second reason for the confidence in the accuracy of the Old Testament is that it includes some accounts which describe the failure and mistakes of very important people. For example, we read that God needed to discipline the Prophet Moses because he had become angry with the people. The sad stories of Aaron and the golden calf, the Prophet Abraham telling a half lie about his wife, and David committing adultery with Bathsheba are all included. If the disciples who preserved these accounts had wanted to change anything, then these sad stories of the failures of Moses, Aaron, Abraham, and David would not have been included in the record.

The fact that moral failure is included in the Old Testament is evidence that the writers were careful not to change the contents. They recognized that all of the Holy Writings needed to be carefully preserved because through them God had begun to reveal Himself to mankind.

A third reason for confidence in the Old Testament as we have it today is the abundance of ancient Old Testament manuscripts which scholars can study and compare with our modern Hebrew texts. The evidence from ancient manuscripts is exceedingly significant. We turn now to a discussion of this important aspect of Biblical scholarship.

Ancient Manuscripts

The Hebrew Old Testament as we have it today is based on a text which comes from a fine Hebrew manuscript which was completed by Aaron ben Asher in A.D. 1008. Aaron ben Asher was an excellent scholar who spent many years studying ancient Hebrew manuscripts of the Old Testament, and his manuscript is the scholarly product of his intense research.

The most ancient complete Hebrew Old Testament in existence today is a manuscript copied by Aaron ben Asher from the famous Aleppo manuscript of his grandfather Moses ben Asher of about A.D. 930. This manuscript is known as the Leningrad (1) Hebrew manuscript. This ben Asher manuscript was copied from the ancient Hebrew Masoretic texts which came directly from the ancient Hebrews of Palestine.

Although our Old Testament is based on the ben Asher Old Testament which comes to us through the ancient Masoretic texts of Palestine, the scholars attempt to determine whether it is an accurate representation of the original writings. The method which is used to determine the accuracy of the present text is comparison with other ancient texts.

There are several sources for these ancient texts:

-- the Greek Septuagint, which is a Greek translation of the Hebrew Old Testament, done in Alexandria, Egypt. This massive translation project involved many translators and took nearly 150 years to complete (285-135 B.C.).

-- an ancient Samaritan version of the *Taurat.*

-- the oldest Latin translation of the Old Testament (second century A.D.).

-- the Syrian translation (second or third centuries A.D.).

-- The Latin Vulgate of Jerome (end of fourth century A.D.). Interestingly there are more than 8,000 manuscripts still in existence of the Latin Vulgate. Obviously the science of textual comparison does not suffer from a lack of manuscripts!

There is another source for comparative textual study which is exceedingly significant. This is the Dead Sea Scrolls discovered by some Bedouin Arabs at Qumran in 1947. These scrolls were found in sealed jars hidden in dry caves close to the Dead Sea in Palestine and the scrolls had been remarkably preserved for over 2,000 years.

The scrolls were copied between 250 and 175 B.C. which is about the same time as the ancient Greek Septuagint was being translated from the Hebrew Old Testament in Alexandria. This remarkable discovery gives scholars access to Old Testament manuscripts dating approximately two centuries before the time of Christ.

These scrolls are preserved in the Jerusalem Museum.

The Dead Sea Scrolls form a tremendous wealth of manuscripts which include 10 complete scrolls and about 600 separate manuscripts, plus thousands of fragments. Consequently, we now have complete manuscripts or fragments of all of the Old Testament books except Esther.

Thus our manuscript evidence of the Old Testament is moved approximately 1,000 years closer to the time the Old Testament was written by the discovery of these scrolls. These manuscripts have shown that the Old Testament as we have it today is an accurate transmission of the Hebrew original.

Some of the caves at Qumran where the Dead Sea Scrolls were discovered. Old Testament manuscripts were found in sealed jars. Some of these manuscripts were copied about 200 B.C.

The first portion of the *Taurat* of the Prophet Moses: notice that the text is in the Hebrew language, which is the language of the Prophet Moses himself. The oldest Hebrew manuscripts of portions of the *Taurat* available today are more than 2,000 years old.

33

Trustworthy Scriptures

Truly God has wonderfully preserved the Holy writings of the prophets![4]

> The Qur'an affirms that God will not permit His Holy Scriptures to be changed.
> The Qur'an says: "no change can there be in the Words of God" *(Yunus* (10): 64).

The Bible says that God will never permit His Word to be destroyed.

> -- The Torah *(Taurat)* of the Prophet Moses frequently refers to the law of God as being "Forever" or everlasting.'
> -- The Psalms *(Zabur)* of the Prophet David says: "Forever, 0 Lord, Thy word is firmly fixed in the heavens" (Psalm 119:89).
> --The Gospel *(Injil)* of Jesus the Messiah says: "Scripture cannot be broken..." (John 10:35).

These and other verses from the Bible itself show that God, who inspired the writing of the Holy Book, also protects the Holy Scriptures. God Himself has always been present protecting His Word.

We can be confident that the Old Testament which we have today is trustworthy. It is an accurate transmission of the Hebrew original, the language of the Prophet Moses himself. But the work of scholars never ceases. They continually compare these ancient manuscripts to make sure that the Old Testament we possess today is in agreement with the originals.

The Dead Sea Scrolls and other ancient manuscripts are a marvelous confirmation that the printed Old Testament

Scriptures, which we have in our possession today, are accurate and reliable.

Modern Biblical scholarship is confident that the Old Testament we have is an accurate record of the revelations of God which have been spoken or written by the holy prophets and their disciples and also that the Holy Scriptures are an accurate description of God's action in the history of the Covenant People. When we read the Old Testament, we can be confident that we are reading an accurate and reliable transmission of the same Holy Scriptures which were recorded through the divine inspiration of the ancient prophets of God such as Moses, David, or Isaiah.

Questions

(1) Who is the great prophet of the *Taurat*?

(2) Describe the Writings and the Prophets.

(3) Who was the Prophet Isaiah?

(4) Give three reasons for confidence in the reliability of the Old Testament Scriptures.

(5) What is the significance of the Dead Sea Scrolls for the study of the Old Testament texts?

3: The New Testament

'And the Word became flesh and dwelt among us, full of grace and truth '. The *Injil* of Jesus the Messiah (John 1:14a).

———————

The central truth of the New Testament is the Gospel *(Injil)* of Jesus the Messiah. The word Gospel or *Injil* means Good News. The New Testament is the Good News that the Messiah whom the prophets had spoken about has come. For this reason the New Testament is a fulfillment of the Old Testament.

In the Old Testament the coming of the Messiah is promised. In the New Testament that promise for a fuller revelation of God through the Messiah is fulfilled through the life, death, and resurrection of Jesus the Messiah.

Our study of the New Testament includes a description of the way in which these Holy Writings of God were recorded and an examination of evidence for the reliability of the New Testament Scriptures in our possession today. First, we need to understand who the men of God were who recorded these Holy Scriptures.

Apostolic writings

Early in the ministry of Jesus the Messiah, He called twelve disciples to be His closest associates (Matthew 10:1-4). One of these twelve disciples, Judas Iscariot, betrayed Jesus, but the other eleven disciples were called by God to become apostles *(rusul)*. Later, after His death and resurrection, the risen Messiah appeared to Paul. God also called Paul to become an apostle.

Others were also called by God to become apostles, but those whom we know best are the Apostle Paul and the eleven faithful disciples (Simon Peter, John, James the son of Zebedee, Andrew, Philip, Bartholomew, Thomas, Matthew, James the son of Alphaeus, Thaddeus, and Simon the Canaanite). After the death and resurrection of Jesus the Messiah the apostles continued the work which the Messiah had begun.

The apostles knew the Messiah. They were witnesses of His life, teachings, crucifixion, and glorious resurrection. The Apostle John wrote:

> "That which was from the beginning, which we have heard, which we have seen with our eyes, which we have looked upon and touched with our hands, concerning the word of life. The life was made manifest, and we saw it, and testify to it, and proclaim to you the eternal life which was with the Father and was made manifest to us--that which we have seen and heard we proclaim also to you" (1 John 1:1-3a).

The apostles are trustworthy witnesses!

For this reason the Church relied on the apostles for their knowledge about the Messiah and His teachings. The writings of the apostles concerning Jesus the Messiah were recognized as God's authoritative Word. The New Testament consists of these apostolic writings.

Within the experience of the Church, the belief in the authority of the apostles who knew the Messiah became very important when decisions needed to be made as to which books to include in the New Testament Scriptures.

When it was written

One of the most interesting aspects of Biblical scholarship is the question concerning when the various books of the New Testament were written.

Some of the most recent scholarship is telling us that it is unlikely that any of the New Testament books were written after AD. 70. It was in that year that the Roman army under the generalship of Tutus destroyed the temple in Jerusalem. This tremendously important event is not mentioned in any of the New Testament books, except for several prophecies which Jesus gave concerning the destruction of the temple.

These prophecies of Jesus took place about 40 years before the temple was destroyed. If these prophecies had been put in writing after the destruction of the temple, the writers would probably have made special mention that such a disaster is proof that Jesus was able to prophesy future events. But the manner in which the prophecies are written shows that they were written before the destruction of the temple in AD. 70.[5]

A recent archeological discovery is also very helpful in determining the dates for a good portion of the New Testament. A small fragment of writing has been found by archeological digging near the city of Corinth in Greece which shows that the Roman Governor Gallio arrived in Corinth in the summer of A.D. 51. In the New Testament Book of Acts we read that the Apostle Paul was also in Corinth at the same time that Gallio was there. (Acts 18:12-17).

Therefore, this fragment of writing which the archaeologists have discovered has made it possible for scholars to date precisely many of the events in the early Church, and also the date for the writing of quite a number of books of the New Testament, because we now know that it was in A.D. 51 that the Apostle Paul's experiences in Corinth took place. Moving backwards and forwards from that date, we can know with considerable certainty when other events also took place.[6]

There are other factors also which help scholars place the dates for the writing of the various New Testament books. But the two most significant clues as to when the books were written are:

(1) The destruction of the temple in Jerusalem in A.D. 70 which seems to have taken place after the writing of the New Testament.

(2) The discovery of a pottery fragment near Corinth which reveals the date (A.D. 51) for Paul's visit to Corinth, and consequently gives a solid clue concerning the general chronological development of the New Testament.

These are two points of evidence which lead us to believe that all of the books of the New Testament were written within the life time of many of the apostles *(rusul)* of God who were disciples of Jesus the Messiah.

Some of the apostles died or were martyred before the destruction of the temple. For example, the Apostle James was martyred in A.D. 43. But many of the apostles lived for many years after the death and resurrection of the Messiah. They had time to teach and write about the Gospel *(Injil)* event under the inspiration of God.

The formation of the New Testament

A problem developed very early in the experience of the Church which forced it to make decisions about the New Testament Scriptures.

The problem was that many books and letters began to circulate in the Church concerning the life and teachings of the Messiah. Many of these were not written by apostles. Some were very legendary. Some writers made up interesting stories concerning Jesus and added to His teachings.

There was, for example, a new philosophy called Gnosticism, which held that salvation is found through hidden knowledge. It taught that the Messiah was not a true man; it taught that He was an illusion, a sort of angel who appeared for a while and then disappeared at the time of His crucifixion.

This problem forced the Church to decide which writings should be included in the New Testament. Christians believe that the Holy Spirit of God led the early Church to the truth just as Jesus the Messiah had promised: ' But the Counsellor, the Holy Spirit, Whom the Father will send in My name, He will teach you all things, and bring to your remembrance all that I have said to you ' (John 14:26).

Three principals were involved in making the decision about which books and letters to include in the New Testament:

(1) Did the writing come through an apostle of God who was a disciple of Jesus the Messiah or through an associate of an apostle?

(2) Was the writing in harmony with the life, teaching, and experience of the Church as formed and begun

by the apostles of God who were disciples of Jesus the Messiah?

(3) Did the writings show the authority of the Spirit of God?

These three tests for inspiration helped the Church as a whole to form a consensus as to which books to include in the New Testament. In fact, the Church only needed officially to accept Scriptures which were already widely accepted throughout the Church. When the leaders of the ancient Church compiled an official list of books to be accepted by the Church as the inspired New Testament Scriptures, the list which they formed consisted of the books and letters which were already being used by the Church as a whole as Holy Scriptures.

This process of selection was completed about A.D. 200. When these Holy Writings were compiled into the New Testament by the Church leaders, the decision was apparently happily accepted throughout the Church.

It is important to recognize that although a final official decision about which books and letters should be included in the New Testament was not completed until about A.D. 200, all of the Scripture portions of the New Testament were written much earlier and all were written by apostles or close associates of apostles.

We have already noted that some portions of the New Testament were written almost immediately after the death and resurrection of the Messiah, and all were completed within the life time of at least some of the apostles who had lived and worked with Jesus the Messiah.

We turn now to a discussion of the content and organization of the New Testament.

The Gospel *(Injil)*

We have already mentioned that the Gospel *(Injil)* is the central truth of the New Testament. The *Injil* is Jesus the Messiah; it is the Good News of the life, teachings, death, and resurrection of the Messiah.

The *Injil* is not only the teachings of the Messiah. The *Injil* also consists of His life, His actions, His death, His resurrection, because God has revealed through His apostles that the Messiah Himself is God's living, eternal Word. Therefore the spoken words as well as the deeds of the Messiah are the content of the *Injil* .

> -- The Qur'an affirms that the coming of the Messiah is Good News. *(Ali Imran (3):45.)*
>
> -- The Qur'an also says concerning the Gospel:
> ·Therein was guidance and light and confirmation of the law *(Taurat)* that had come before him: a guidance and an admonition' *(Maida (5):49).*

The Holy Writings which are called the *Injil* consist of four books, each of which was written by one of Jesus' faithful disciples. The books which these disciples have written are called Matthew, Mark, Luke and John, which are the names of the four holy men of God who were responsible for the writing of these four books.

In other words, the book called Matthew is the record of the life and teachings of the Messiah as recorded by Matthew who was an apostle of God and a disciple of Jesus the Messiah. He places great emphasis on the fact that Jesus the Messiah fulfills the promises of God given through the prophets of the Old Testament. In Matthew

5:17 we read that the Messiah said: "Think not that I have come to abolish the law and the prophets; I have not come to abolish, but to fulfil them."

The second book is Mark. The traditions tell us that Mark was a close associate of the Apostle Peter who was one of the disciples who worked most closely with Jesus the Messiah during His ministry. We believe that Mark wrote the Gospel record under the guidance of the Apostle Peter and the inspiration of the Holy Spirit.

Luke is the third book of the New Testament. It was written by Luke, who was a medical doctor who travelled and worked closely with the Apostle Paul. Luke sensed the need for a record of the *Injil* to be written which would pay a great deal of attention to historical details. Luke worked with the Apostle Paul to write that book.

Luke states that the purpose for his writing is that, "It seemed good to me also, having followed all things closely for some time past, to write an orderly account for you most excellent Theophilus, that you may know the truth concerning the things of which you have been informed" (Luke 1:3,4).

Under the guidance and inspiration of God, Luke certainly did fulfil that goal! He seems to have interviewed carefully people who had been close to Jesus the Messiah, including Jesus' own mother, the Virgin Mary. Archeology and present day research have established that Luke was a very accurate historian.[7]

The fourth book is John. The Apostle John was the closest disciple to the Messiah. He is sometimes referred to as the disciple whom Jesus loved, and he understood keenly the thought of the Messiah. Borne along by the inspiring power of God, he sensed in a profound way the deep meaning of the coming of the Messiah.

The first three books of the New Testament have certain similarities. Because of the similarity in content, these three books are called the Synoptic Gospels.

Nevertheless, all four of the gospel *(Injil)* writers, Matthew, Mark, Luke, and John, were witnesses to the glory and saving presence of Jesus the Messiah within human history. Each writer presents a profound description of Jesus the Messiah. They all wrote so that we may know with certainty that the Messiah is God's eternal Word and that through Him there is eternal salvation.

The *Injil* recorded by John says that these Scriptures are written "...that you may believe that Jesus is the Christ (Messiah), the Son of God,* and that believing you may have life in His name ' (John 20:31).

The Acts and Epistles

The fifth book of the New Testament is called the Acts of the Apostles. This is a history of the early Church. It describes the day of Pentecost when the Church was created by the Holy Spirit. Acts goes on to describe significant aspects of the first thirty years of Church history.

Luke is the writer of the Acts, and this book has the same characteristic of attention to detail which is true of the third book of the *Injil* recorded by Luke. His close association with the Apostle Paul is very important in the writing of the Acts of the Apostles.

---

* The title Son of God is one of the names which God gave to the Messiah in the Injil. It shows that the Messiah had a perfect relationship with God and that God has chosen to reveal Himself fully in the Messiah. It shows that the Messiah is the Living Word of God.

This book is not only a fascinating history of the early apostolic   Church, but also a profound revelation of the saving power of the risen Messiah in the life of the Church. A number of sermons by apostolic leaders are recorded in the Acts. These sermons reveal the basic meaning of the life, death, and resurrection of Jesus the Messiah.

The remainder of the New Testament consists of letters and teachings by the apostles of God, or close associates of the apostles. Some of these letters were written to particular churches. For example, Ephesians was a letter written by the Apostle Paul to the Church at Ephesus, in Asia Minor. Hebrews describes the Messiah as the glorious fulfillment of the Old Testament. It interprets the meaning of the sacrificial offering of animals as a sign of the death and resurrection of Jesus the Messiah. Another letter by James describes good Christian conduct. James was from the family of Jesus, and was leader of the Church in Jerusalem. All the letters to the churches give instructions concerning right belief and practice in the Church.

Other letters were written to Church leaders to instruct them on the manner in which they should conduct themselves. For example, there are two letters written by the Apostle Paul to a young leader called Timothy, instructing him on the manner in which to lead the Christians in his area. Another letter called Philemon is a fascinating little document written by the Apostle Paul asking a slave master to love his slave and treat him as his own brother . Probably the slave master freed his slave after receiving that letter from an apostle of   God!

The names of the letters, sometimes called epistles, are as follows: Romans, 1 and 2 Corinthians, Galatians, Ephesians, Philippians, Colossians, 1and 2 Thessalonians, 1and 2 Timothy, Titus, Philemon, Hebrews, James, 1 and 2 Peter, 1, 2 and 3 John and Jude.

Revelation is the final part of the New Testament. This book of teachings is a glorious drama portraying the struggle of the forces of evil with the Church, and the ultimate triumph of Jesus, the glorified Messiah, at His second coming.

The Church recognized that these letters and books were inspired Scripture. The believers read them often and kept them carefully.

Divine Inspiration

We have already mentioned that the New Testament was written by apostles of God, or their associates. The apostles knew Jesus the Messiah. We know that secondhand information is never as accurate as firsthand information.[8] The apostles of God who were disciples of Jesus the Messiah lived and worked with Him.

The New Testament Scriptures which God inspired these holy apostles to write were based on what the apostles heard and saw as they lived with Jesus. We believe that the witness of these apostles of God is true.

A second reason for confidence in the New Testament is the evidence of archeology and the writings and records of people who lived at the time of Jesus. There is, for example, The *History of the Jewish People*, written by Flavius Josephus during the same century as the New Testament was written.

By comparing the historical detail in the New Testament with evidence from sources outside of the New Testament, scholars can test the reliability of the New Testament records. From these sources of evidence outside the New Testament, scholars have found that the cultural, historical and geographical detail of the New Testament is accurate.[9]

The writers of the New Testament were not characterized by carelessness. Although they lived in a complex political situation, they reported relevant events with astonishing accuracy. Different titles for political leaders such as King, proconsul, high priest, strategoi, politarchs, Asiarchs, or governors are accurately presented. Geographical details such as the names of places or city streets, the descriptions of topography or climate are also accurate.

If the New Testament writers were careful not to make mistakes in "little" details, surely they were also accurate in their descriptions of more important details such as the miracles of Jesus the Messiah, His teachings, His crucifixion, His resurrection and Pentecost, when the Church was created.[10]

A third and most important reason for confidence in the New Testament is our confidence in God Himself. Jesus the Messiah was absolutely sure that His teachings were the eternal Word of God.

The Messiah declared, "Heaven and earth will pass away, but My words will not pass away" (Matthew 24:35).

The apostles of God who recorded the words of the Messiah and to whom God revealed the meaning of the life, death and resurrection of Jesus the Messiah were also certain that they were speaking and writing God's revealed Word.

The Apostle Paul writes, ' What no eye has seen, nor ear heard, nor the heart of man conceived what God has prepared for those who love him, God has revealed to us through the Spirit ' (1 Corinthians 2:9, 10).

At another place, the Apostle Paul writes that his teachings come from "the Lord" (1 Corinthians 7:10).

Again we read, "But even if we, or an angel from heaven, should preach to you a Gospel contrary to that which we preached to you, let him be accursed" (Galatians 1:8)!

The Apostle Peter refers to the first writings which form the New Testament as the Good News preached to you "through the Holy Spirit sent from Heaven, things into which angels long to look" (1 Peter 1:12). This astonishing verse suggests that God's revelation through the Messiah which is recorded in the New Testament is a more perfect revelation than the angels know!

In the last chapter of the New Testament it is written, "I warn everyone who hears the words of the prophecy of this book: If anyone adds to them, God will add to him the plagues described in this book, and if anyone takes away from the words of the book of this prophecy, God will take away his share in the tree of life and in the holy city, which are described in this book" (Revelation 22:18, 19).

This terrible warning at the end of the New Testament was always accepted with great seriousness by the early Church. The Church knows that it is a sin against God to change His Word. All of the New Testament writings need to be respected and accepted as God's Word which has been revealed to us in Jesus the Messiah and recorded through divine inspiration by the apostles of God.

Ancient Manuscripts

The original New Testament texts were written in the Greek language. We need to know whether the Greek New Testament as we have it today is an accurate transmission of the original writings. Is the Greek New Testament reliable which scholars use as a basis of all translation work into other languages? Is the Greek New Testament which the scholars have used as a basis for the translations into Arabic, Swahili, or English an accurate copy of the original Greek manuscripts which were written through the inspiration of God?

Scholars are overwhelmed by the abundance of New Testament Greek manuscripts. More than 5,000 ancient manuscripts are available: 81 papyri, 25 ostraca (pieces of pottery on which fragments of Greek text are to be found), 250 unicals (manuscripts written in capital letters). All of these date from before the 10th century AD. From the 10th century to the 15th century the manuscripts include nearly 2,000 miniscules (Greek written in flowing hand-writing) and 3,000 lectionaries (manuscripts copied especially for public worship service). At least 50 of these ancient manuscripts are complete with no portion lost or defaced! Scholars are overwhelmed by the abundance of material.

Scholars are not satisfied with just an abundance of manuscripts. They try to find the most ancient manuscripts possible so as to establish the most accurate possible Greek text. The work of scholars in this regard was greatly aided by a fantastic discovery which occurred in Egypt during some archaeological investigations which began in 1897 near Oxyrhnchus.

While digging at Oxyrhnchus, a workman accidentally hit a mummified crocodile with his spade, and the mummy broke open. To the astonishment of everyone the mummy was hollow, and inside the crocodile mummy they found waste paper (pieces of old papyrus with writing on it).

The papyrus included hundreds of written documents from before the time of Jesus the Messiah and also after the beginning of the Christian era. There were more than 75 manuscripts of portions of the New Testament.

The most significant document in the crocodile was a

fragment of the Gospel *(Injil)* as recorded by the Apostle John, which is dated at about A.D. 135.This is the most ancient portion of the New Testament which has ever been discovered by modern man. This manuscript is now preserved in the John Rylands Library in Manchester, England.

The crocodile story is not the only remarkable event in the discovery of ancient Biblical manuscripts. We have already noted the tremendous significance for Old Testament studies of the discovery of the Dead Sea Scrolls. New Testament textual studies also have been greatly helped by a number of surprising discoveries similar to that of the mummified crocodile stuffed with papyrus manuscripts.

C. Von Tischendorf's finding of the Sinaiticus manuscripts is another example of a surprising discovery. Tischendorf was one of the greatest manuscript hunters. This 19th century scholar gave a lifetime to looking for and analyzing ancient Biblical manuscripts. His search took him on repeated trips to the Middle East where the world's most ancient Christian churches and monasteries are to be found.

It was at Mount Sinai in the Sinai Desert that Tischendorf made his most significant discovery. At the Monastery of St. Catherine, on the side of the same mountain from which God had revealed the Ten Commandments to the Prophet Moses, Tischendorf found containers of old paper which the monks were using to start their fires. He found that the paper contained pages from ancient Greek New Testament manuscripts which the Coptic-speaking monks could not read. He begged them to stop burning the manuscripts.

After further visits, these Christian desert monks permitted Tischendorf to study the manuscripts thoroughly. The collection dates from the fourth century A.D., and is known today as the Sinaiticus manuscripts. In

1933 the Sinaiticus collection was brought to the British Museum where it is being carefully preserved.

Trustworthy Scriptures

The first Greek New Testament was printed early in the 16th century shortly after the invention of printing. This printed text was based on eleventh century manuscripts which had been copied and transmitted from the Byzantine Text which was the standard New Testament text used in Constantinople, Turkey, as early as A.D. 380.

Scholars believe the Byzantine Text originated in Antioch, Syria, which was an early Apostolic Church center. It is significant that the first printed Greek New Testament text derives from the manuscripts used in Turkey and Syria only some three hundred years after the original texts were written.

Nevertheless, the scholars are determined to investigate textual sources which are even earlier than the Byzantine Text. There are three main sources of pre-Byzantine texts.

First, there are the Alexandrian texts. The two greatest Alexandrian manuscripts date from the fourth century and are known as Vaticanus and Sinaiticus, which we have already mentioned in connection with Tischendorf s discovery at Mount Sinai. These great manuscripts (the Vaticanus and Sinaiticus) are the most reliable pre-Byzantine sources for textual study.

The second source of pre-Byzantine text comes to us through the Roman tradition of the Church and is known as the Western Text.

The third source is the Caesarean texts, which originated in Palestine.

Scholars also investigate ancient translations of the New Testament such as the 2nd century Syriac translation or the 4th century Egyptian and Ethiopian translations. Additional help comes from Biblical quotations from the writings of early Church leaders such as Origen from Egypt, Tertullian from North Africa, Ignatius from Palestine, or Iranaeus of Europe.

Present day New Testament scholars rely much on the Alexandrian manuscripts and to a lesser extent on the Western, Caesarean, and Byzantine Texts. This four-way comparison of ancient texts has greatly increased scholarly ability to develop a truly accurate New Testament Greek text. Scholars assure us that the most refined Greek texts available today are highly reliable.

The Biblical scholar F.J.A. Hort states that the possibility of diversion from the original text is only 00.1%, or one tenth of one percent![11] Even though only 1 out of every 1,000 words or phrases might be slightly variant from the original text, not one of those possible differences possesses any real significance to the message which the Bible conveys.

We need to remember that until the 16th century all New Testament manuscripts were handwritten, and we know that mistakes can occur when copying from one manuscript to another. Therefore, when scholarly investigation of the ancient texts indicates that a word or phrase in the modern Greek text is not exactly the same as the original writings, a notation is made in the printed Greek text so that it can reflect accurately the original Scripture.

The process of ongoing study of the most ancient manuscripts is one reason why translations of the Bible need to be revised sometimes. An example is the King James Version of the English translation of the Bible. This

17th Century English translation was based on a printed Greek text known as the Erasmus Text, which was based on the Byzantine Text. As we have already noted, scholars today have access to texts which are older than the fourth century Byzantine Text, and consequently some small revisions in the Erasmus Text have been necessary.

Bible translators today rely on a Greek text edited by Eberhard Nestle and first printed around the beginning of this century. This printed Greek New Testament is based on the most recent investigations in the ancient texts. It relies heavily on pre-Byzantine texts, especially the Alexandrian manuscripts, and includes notes on other ancient texts to help the Bible translator be sure that he is in closest possible contact with the original manuscripts.

Every reprint of the Nestle Greek New Testament includes the most up-to-date findings of scholars. The Nestle Greek New Testament text (25th edition) is almost identical to that published in 1968 by the United Bible Societies.

Therefore we can be certain that the Greek New Testament we possess today is an accurate transmission of the Scriptures as inspired by God through His apostles.[12]

Questions

(1) What was the role of the apostles in the writing of the New Testament Scriptures?

(2) What is the Gospel (*Injil*)?

(3) What are the Epistles?

(4) How did the early Church decide which books and letters were the inspired Word of God?

(5) Why are ancient manuscripts of the New Testament important?

A portion of the *Injil* as recorded by the Apostle John. Notice that the text is in the Greek language, the same language which all the holy men of God used in writing the New Testament Scriptures. The oldest portion of a manuscript of the *Injil* according to John which is available today is about 1,850 years old.

4: Translations

"But the Word is very near you; it is in your mouth and in your heart, so that you can do it." The *Taurat* of the Prophet Moses. (Deut. 30:14)

The New Testament was written in the Greek language because that was the language of the common person throughout the Middle Eastern World at the time of the Messiah. By writing in Greek, the apostles of the Messiah were able to communicate the Gospel to millions of people in Western Asia, North Africa and Europe. The Greek used by these writers is simple and easy to comprehend, but it is also a very expressive language.

Even today Biblical scholars study Greek so that they can read the New Testament in the language first used by the apostles.

We have already mentioned that the Old Testament was written in Hebrew. Biblical scholars also need to know the Hebrew language in order to read the Old Testament text in its original language.

The Holy Scriptures reveal to us that through Jesus the Messiah, God chose to reveal Himself perfectly and wonderfully in the human community. God's eternal Word, became man, and lived among men. In Jesus the Messiah we see God's eternal Word clothed, in human cultural form (John 1:1, 2, 14).

It is for this reason that the Church has always felt that it is necessary to translate the Bible into the language of people who do not understand the Greek and Hebrew languages. A Bible translation presents the written Word of God in the language of a particular people. It is an attempt to clothe the Gospel in the language culture of a people so that the people can understand and accept the Gospel more readily.

If God chose to reveal Himself in human history and culture through a Man, the Messiah, then the witness of the Church in human society must also be conducted in the language of the people. For this kind of witness to happen, the Scriptures must be available for the people to read in their own language.

> The Qur'an commands the people of the Book not to hide the Holy Scriptures. We read: "And remember, God took a Covenant from the People of the Book, to make it known and clear to mankind, and not to hide it" *(Ali Imran (3): 187).*

Christians attempt to open the Holy Scriptures for people to read and understand by translating the Bible into the languages of people everywhere. Faithful Christians do not desire to hide the Holy Scriptures. They want people everywhere to read, understand and believe the written Word of God.

The early Church began this process of translating the Bible into languages of the people who did not know the Greek and Hebrew languages. The first known translation of the New Testament was completed about 150 years after the time of Jesus the Messiah on earth, and this was a translation from the Greek into the Syrian language of Mesopotamia. Some ancient Syriac translations of the New Testament and Old Testament are still in existence today.

In Africa a cluster of translations was made in Egypt, where the Coptic Church made three translations of the Bible into three different dialects of Egypt. These Egyptian translations of the Bible were probably completed about

250 years after the resurrection of the Messiah.

At about the same time the churches of North Africa (present day Tunisia and Algeria) made the first Latin translation of the Bible. Shortly thereafter the Ethiopians translated the Bible into Geez. The ancient African Christians were remarkably active in translating the Bible into the languages they could understand best.

By the end of the fourth century A.D. the process of Bible translation into the languages of peoples who did not understand the Greek language had already progressed significantly in Asia, Africa, and Europe. The process of Bible translation has continued right up to the present day.

Even the most remote peoples today are receiving the Bible in their own language through the dedicated efforts of linguistic scholars. The whole Bible, or parts of it, is now available in more than 2,000 languages!

Questions

(1) What was the original language of the Old Testament? The New Testament?

(2) Why do Christians translate the Bible into so many different languages?

Conclusion

No other ancient writings have such a wealth of manuscripts available for scholarly study as does the Bible.[13] For example; scholars possess only one copy of a manuscript of *The Annals* by Cornelius Tacitus, written about the end of the first century A.D. That one manuscript is a ninth century A.D. manuscript. Tacitus was one of the most significant Roman historians! Yet only one manuscript survives! And that one manuscript was copied about 800 years after the writing of the original *Annals*!

For the New Testament, some of which was written before Tacitus was born, we have over 5,000 manuscripts; the oldest fragment is dated about A.D. 135! This is astonishing! Similarly, the Dead Sea Scrolls have given scholars access to a wealth of Old Testament manuscripts which were first copied more than 2,000 years ago. No other ancient book is supported by such a tremendous amount and quality of ancient manuscripts as is the Bible. Surely God has had His hand in all of this!

Jesus the Messiah said, ' Heaven and earth shall pass away, but My Word shall not pass away· (Matthew 24:35).

The Prophet David said much the same thing, ' Forever, 0 Lord, Thy Word is firmly fixed in the heavens' (Psalm 119:89).

Through the holy prophets and apostles God has inspired the writing of the Holy Scriptures. God has also protected these writings throughout the centuries so that when we read God's wonderful Word today we can be confident that the Holy Scriptures are indeed God's revelation to us and to all people.

It is encouraging to know that the Bible we have today is trustworthy. But it is equally important to know what the

Holy Book of God says. The Holy Scriptures become a blessing to us when we respond in faith, repentance, and obedience to the Living Word of God. We should read the Holy Book of God, and, we need to open our lives to the Living Word of God, who is the Messiah.

Jesus the Messiah said: "...search the Scriptures; ...it is they that bear witness to Me" (John 5:39)!

Appendix A

Comments from the Qur'an concerning the Bible

Some Muslims fear that the Bible is not trustworthy because they suspect that it has been corrupted. It is noteworthy that the Qur'an never accuses Christians of corrupting the Scriptures.

The Qur'an does accuse some People of the Book of distorting the Scriptures with their mouths when they interpret it:

> "There is among them a section that distorts the Book with their tongues; (As they read) you would think it is a part of the Book, but it is not part of the Book, and they say, 'That is from God,' but it is not from God; it is they who tell a lie against God, and well they know it" (Ali Imran (3); aya 78)!

The Qur'an does appeal to the Christians and Jews not to hide their Scriptures:

> "Ye People of the Book! Why do ye clothe-with falsehood, and conceal the Truth, while ye have knowledge" (Ali lmran (3): aya 71)!

The Qur'an does warn against writing false Scriptures:

> "Then woe to those who write the Book with their own hands, and then say: "This is from God," to traffic with it for a miserable price!

-- Woe to them for what their hands do write and for the gain they make thereby" (Baqara (2): aya 79).

It is true that during the history of the Church some Christians interpreted the Bible wrongly with their mouths, but the study of ancient manuscripts of the Bible assures us that the texts in our possession today are accurate. The Church has always tried accurately to preserve the written words of Scripture. The Bible itself is not corrupted.

It is also true that some Christians do not give the Holy Scriptures to others as freely as they should; that is to say, they hide or conceal the Scriptures. Nevertheless, we also know that the Church as a whole is concerned about making the Bible available to everyone everywhere. In fact, it is for this reason that the Bible or portions of it have already been translated into 2,000 languages.

It is true that some false scriptures have been written. The Gospel of Barnabas is a modern example of false scriptures. It is a fourteenth century invention which distorts both the New Testament and the Qur'an. The Qur'an condemns those who write and circulate false scriptures.

We know that the Bible itself does not contain false scriptures. The ancient Church determined not to include any false scriptures in the Old Testament or the New Testament. Only those Holy Scriptures which had been inspired by God through the apostles were included in the New Testament.

We are certain that God Himself who inspired the writing of the Old and New Testament Scriptures also protected those Scriptures so that no false scriptures were included.

The Qur'an gives repeated witness that the Word of God cannot be corrupted. For example, we read:

> "Rejected were the Apostles before thee; with patience and constancy they bore their rejection and their wrongs, until our aid did reach them; there is none that can alter the Words and Decrees of God" (Anam (6): aya 34).

This verse shows that even though people may reject God's revelation through the apostles, God Himself will protect that revelation. God's Word cannot be changed. God Himself protects His Word.

Elsewhere the Qur'an says:

> "No change can there be in the Words of God" (Yunus (10): aya 64).

A tradition noted by Bukhari (Book, ar-Rad) affirms that the Holy Scriptures are not corrupted. He writes:

> "'They corrupt the word" means "they alter or change its meaning." Yet no one is able to change even a single word from any Book of God. The meaning is that they interpret the word wrongly."[14]

Neither the Qur'an nor the traditions of Islam, when carefully studied, support the notion that the Bible is corrupted. In fact, both give witness that the Scriptures are true and that the Bible is for all humankind.

The Qur'an says: ' And remember God took a Covenant from the People of the Book, to make it known and clear to humankind, and not to hide it ' (Ali Imran (3): aya 187). Both the *Taurat* and the *Injil* are called a ' guidance and a light ' to mankind (Maida (5): ayat 47, 49). Even Mohammed is commanded by God to go to the People of the Book when in doubt: 'If thou wert in doubt as to what we have revealed unto thee, then ask those who have been reading the Book from before thee..." (Yunus 10: aya 94).

Appendix B

The history of the Holy Book of God

Approximate
Dates

2000 B.C.	-The Prophet Abraham
1300 B.C.	-The Prophet Moses and the Priest and Prophet Aaron
1000 B.C.	-The Prophet David
450 B.C.	-The Priest Ezra -Organization of the Writings and the Prophets
400-300 B.C.	-Last Portion of the Old Testament written
300-200 B.C.	-The Old Testament canon*comple ted
285-135 B.C.	-The Translation of the Septuagint (Greek Old Testament)
200 B.C.	-The oldest available Old Testament manuscripts
6 B.C.	-Jesus the Messiah born
AD. 40-A.D. 70	-The New Testament written

---

* Canon means list. It is the list of books included in the Old Testament and New Testament.

65

A.D. 135	-The oldest available New Testament manuscripts
A.D. 200	-The New Testament canon decided. -The first translations of the New Testament from Greek into other languages.
A.D. 1500	Beginning of wide-spread use of printing.
A.D. 1995	Bibles or portions of the Bible translated into more than 2,000 languages

For further reading

Albright, W.F., *From the Stone Age to Christianity*, New
       York, Doubleday, 1957

Brown, David, *The Christian Scriptures*, London, Sheldon
       Press, 1968

Bruce, F. F., *The New Testament Documents*,
       Leicester, England, IVP, 1976

Dodd, C. H., *The Authority of the Bible*, New York, Harper,
       1962

Hahn, Ernest, *The Integrity of the Bible According to the
       Qur'an and the Hadith*, Henry Martyn Institute of
       Islamic Studies, Hyderabad, India, 1977

Jadeed, Iskander, *The Infallibility of the Torah and the
       Gospel*, Center for Young Adults, Basel,
       Switzerland, n.d.

Jomier, J., *Jesus, the Life of the Messiah*, Park Town,
       Madras, India, CLS, 1974

Kealy, Sean, *The Changing Bible*, Nairobi, KUC, n.d.

Miller, Donald G., *The Authority of the Bible*,
       Grand Rapids, Michigan, Eerdmans, 1972 Moulton,

Harold K., *Papyrus, Parchment, andPrint*,
       London, Lutterworth Press, 1967

Neil, S., *The Interpretation of the NewTestament*, London,
       Oxford, 1966

Richardson, A., *The Bible in the Age of Science*, London,
       SCM, 1968

Robinson, John A. T., *Redating the New Testament*,
       London, SCM, 1976

Ryan, M. R., *Contemporary New Testament Studies*,
       Collegeville, The Liturgical Press, 1965

Smartha, S. J. and Taylor, J. B., eds., *Christian-Muslim
       Dialogue, Papers Presented at the Broumara
       Consultation, 12-18July, 1972*, Geneva, W.C.C.,
       1973

Snaith, Norman H., *The Inspiration and Authority of the
       Bible*, London Epworth, 1958

Wenger, J. C., *God's Word Written*, Scottdale, Herald
       Press, 1968

End notes

[1] J. C. Wenger, *God's Word Written*, Scottdale, Herald Press, 1968, 30.

[2] W. F. Albright, From the Stone Age to Christianity, New York, Doubleday, 1957, 249, 272.

[3] Ibid., 11-17.

[4] Wenger, 109.

[5] John A. T. Robinson, *Redating the New Testament*, London, SCM, 1975, 13-30.

[6] Ibid., 31-32.

[7] F. F. Bruce, *The New Testament Documents,* IVP, Leicester, England, 1976, 41-46.

[8] Robinson, 336-358.

[9] S. Neil, *The Interpretation of the New Testament*, London, Oxford, 1966, 142.

[10] Bruce, 93-99.

[11] Sean Kealy, *The Changing Bible*, Nairobi, K.U.C., N.D., 87.

[12] Wenger, 114-116.

[13] Kealy, 86.

[14] Ernest Hahn, *The Integrity of the Bible According to the Qur'an and the Hadith*, Henry Martyn Institute of Islamic Studies, Hyderabad, India, 1977, 38.

Made in the USA
Charleston, SC
02 December 2016